I0428599

A Little Book of Christmas

An Abundance of Quotes for the Festive Season

Alicia Brent

ISBN-13: 978-1503366282
ISBN-10: 1503366286

Introduction

What do you think about Christmas time?

For some it has religious significance and is an opportunity for reflection, for others it's a time for partying and family get-togethers. For lots of us it's a time of warm-hearted giving and receiving as well as eating too much, drinking a bit more than usual and being generally merry. The season may be tinged with sadness or full of joy. Many thoroughly enjoy Christmas whilst others absolutely detest the very mention of it.

It's certainly one of the few times we ever bring an entire tree into our houses, offices and hospitals.

As Christmas draws nearer people tend to smile more often and dip deeply into their pockets for those less fortunate than themselves. Children's faces light up with excitement and anticipation, whilst parents forage for presents to wrap and be rewarded later by watching the delight on little faces and listening to squeals of happiness as their children rip the paper off hoped-for presents on the big day.

Are you someone who shops early on (possibly throughout the year whenever you spot a bargain gift); plans carefully so that you can be somewhat more relaxed in the run-up to Christmas Day? Or are you among those who rush frantically to the shops at the eleventh hour to get that last minute present for auntie Flo or, hopefully, pick up an excellent deal on a reduced-price turkey?

If you go around a supermarket shortly before closing time on Christmas Eve you're sure to see dozens of almost empty shelves, making it look like everyone's stocked their kitchen cupboards for a whole year instead of a couple of days.

Whatever your view of Christmas, I hope you enjoy this bumper collection of thoughts about it, many from the famous and a few from the not so famous –comedians, actors, singers, writers, politicians... It's a mixed bag of comments - funny, informative, thought-provoking, even controversial.

Happy reading everyone!

Mail your packages early so the post office can lose them in time for Christmas.

Johnny Carson

Christmas waves a magic wand over this world, and behold, everything is softer and more beautiful.

Norman Vincent Peale

I stopped believing in Santa Claus when my mother took me to see him in a department store, and he asked for my autograph.

Shirley Temple

I like the idea of putting your Christmas wish list up and letting people share it.

Bill Gates

He who has not Christmas in his heart will never find it under a tree.

Roy L. Smith

Christmas is a season for kindling the fire for hospitality in the hall, the genial flame of charity in the heart.

Washington Irving

Happy, happy Christmas, that can win us back to the delusions of our childhood days, recall to the old man the pleasures of his youth, and transport the traveler back to his own fireside and quiet home!

Charles Dickens

I once wanted to become an atheist, but I gave up - they have no holidays.

Henny Youngman

Many merry Christmases, friendships, great accumulation of cheerful recollections, affection on earth, and Heaven at last for all of us.

Charles Dickens

Unless we make Christmas an occasion to share our blessings, all the snow in Alaska won't make it 'white'.

Bing Crosby

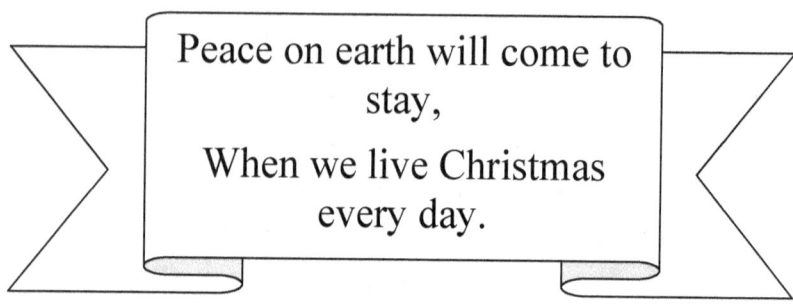

Peace on earth will come to stay,

When we live Christmas every day.

Helen Steiner Rice

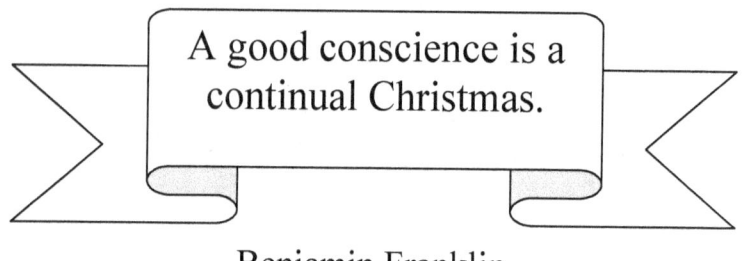

A good conscience is a continual Christmas.

Benjamin Franklin

Moving between the legs of tables and of chairs, rising or falling, grasping at kisses and toys, advancing boldly, sudden to take alarm, retreating to the corner of arm and knee, eager to be reassured, taking pleasure in the fragrant brilliance of the Christmas tree.

T. S. Eliot

Lovely thing about Christmas is that it's compulsory, like a thunderstorm, and we all go through it together.

Garrison Keillor

When we were children
we were grateful to those
who filled our stockings
at Christmas time. Why
are we not grateful to
God for filling our
stockings with legs?

Gilbert K. Chesterton

Pets, like their
owners, tend to
expand a little
over the
Christmas period.

Frances Wright

We consider Christmas as the encounter, the great encounter, the historical encounter, the decisive encounter, between God and mankind. He who has faith knows this truly; let him rejoice.

Pope Paul VI

Let the children have their night of fun and laughter, let the gifts of Father Christmas delight their play. Let us grown-ups share to the full in their unstinted pleasures...

Sir Winston Churchill

> Christmas gives us the opportunity to pause and reflect on the important things around us - a time when we can look back on the year that has passed and prepare for the year ahead.

David Cameron

> At Christmas, I am always struck by how the spirit of togetherness lies also at the heart of the Christmas story. A young mother and a dutiful father with their baby were joined by poor shepherds and visitors from afar. They came with their gifts to worship the Christ child.

Queen Elizabeth II

No matter what, I always make it home for Christmas. I love to go to my Tennessee Mountain Home and invite all of my nieces and nephews and their spouses and kids and do what we all like to do - eat, laugh, trade presents and just enjoy each other... and sometimes I even dress up like Santa Claus!

Dolly Parton

As we give presents at Christmas, we need to recognize that sharing our time and ourselves is such an important part of giving.

Gordon B. Hinckley

When you give up yourself, that's when you will feel the true spirit of Christmas. And that's giving that's serving others and that's when you feel fulfilled.

Joel Osteen

Christ was born in the first century, yet he belongs to all centuries. He was born a Jew, yet He belongs to all races. He was born in Bethlehem, yet He belongs to all countries.

George W. Truett

I detest 'Jingle Bells,' 'White Christmas,' 'Rudolph the Red Nosed Reindeer,' and the obscene spending bonanza that nowadays seems to occupy not just December, but November and much of October, too.

Richard Dawkins

My mother-in-law has come round to our house at Christmas seven years running. This year we're having a change. We're going to let her in.

Les Dawson

I think that 'Ghost Rider: Spirit of Vengeance' was mentally taxing, if only because I had to go to a Christmas party shortly after I had wrapped photography in Romania at two in the morning as the Ghost Rider. The invitation had a Christmas ornament on it with Ghost Rider's face on it as a tree.

Nicolas Cage

On Christmas morning, before we could open our Christmas presents, we would go to this stranger's home and bring them presents. I remember helping clean the house up and putting up a tree. My father believed that you have a responsibility to look after everyone else.

George Clooney

And the Grinch, with his Grinch-feet ice cold in the snow,
Stood puzzling and puzzling, how could it be so?
It came without ribbons. It came without tags.
It came without packages, boxes or bags.
And he puzzled and puzzled 'till his puzzler was sore.
Then the Grinch thought of something he hadn't before.
What if Christmas, he thought, doesn't come from a store.
What if Christmas, perhaps, means a little bit more.

Dr. Seuss

I throw a Christmas party at my house. It's not really a Christmas party, because I don't want to call it a Christmas party. But let's just say I put a lot of Christmas trees around the house, so it smells good

Bill Murray

My mother was a professional sick person; she took a lot of pain pills. There are many people like that. It's just how they are used to getting attention. I always remember she's the daughter of alcoholics who'd leave her alone at Christmas time.

Jim Carrey

I know that a Christmas tree farm in Pennsylvania is about the most random place for a country singer to come from, but I had an awesome childhood.

Taylor Swift

I heard the bells on Christmas Day.
Their old familiar carols play.
And wild and sweet the words repeat.
Of peace on earth goodwill to men.

Henry Wadsworth Longfellow

I've always loved Christmas and that's not really gone away from me from being a child to now. It's always a magical time and I'm unashamed in my love for Christmas.

Martin Freeman

We should declare war on North Vietnam. We could pave the whole country and put parking strips on it, and still be home by Christmas.

Ronald Reagan

I remember a great America where we made everything. There was a time when the only thing you got from Japan was a really bad cheap transistor radio that some aunt gave you for Christmas.

Cher

Christmas it seems to me is a necessary festival; we require a season when we can regret all the flaws in our human relationships: it is the feast of failure, sad but consoling.

Graham Greene

Religious symbols should be visible in public space, in a dignified and non-provocative manner. Christmas trees here, Jewish menorahs there and, further along, a minaret - these symbols represent human life in all its diversity.

Tariq Ramadan

I'm dreaming of a white Christmas,
Just like the ones I used to know,
Where the tree tops glisten
And children listen
To hear sleigh bells in the snow.

Irving Berlin

It always depresses me when people moan about how commercial Christmas is. I love everything about it. The tradition of having this great big feast, slap bang in the middle of winter, is an essential thing to look forward to at the end of the year.

Richard E. Grant

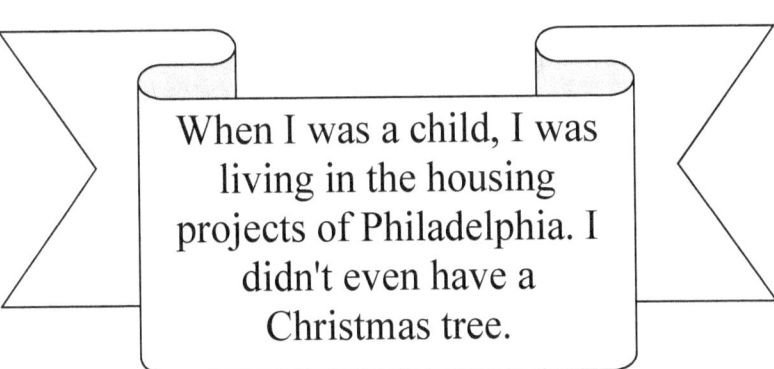

When I was a child, I was living in the housing projects of Philadelphia. I didn't even have a Christmas tree.

Bill Cosby

Ranking among the greatest Christmas movie classics, 'It's a Wonderful Life' tells a beautiful story about the priceless value of relationships.

John C. Maxwell

People can't concentrate properly on blowing other people to pieces if their minds are poisoned by thoughts suitable to the twenty-fifth of December.

Ogden Nash

I suppose if you look back to your early childhood you accept everything people tell you, and that includes a heavy dose of irrationality - you're told about tooth fairies and Father Christmas and things.

Richard Dawkins

It doesn't bother me a bit when people say, 'Merry Christmas' to me. I don't think they are slighting me or getting ready to put me in a ghetto. In fact, I kind of like it.

Ben Stein

Christmas is not a date. It is a state of mind.

Mary Ellen Chase

I didn't know the full dimensions of forever, but I knew it was longer than waiting for Christmas to come.

Richard Brautigan

At the heart of every really good Christmas movie is the threat, I suppose, to Christmas. Something is wrong with Christmas, in all of these movies. In 'The Polar Express,' there's a kid that doesn't really believe, and that's the threat to Christmas. In 'Santa Claus: The Movie,' jealousy and greed are threatening to overrun his Christmas.

James McAvoy

There's nothing sadder in this world than to awake Christmas morning and not be a child.

Erma Bombeck

I still get up every morning at 4 A.M. I write seven days a week, including Christmas. And I still face a blank page every morning, and my characters don't really care how many books I've sold.

Dan Brown

At Christmas play and make good cheer,
For Christmas comes but once a year.

Thomas Tusser

I had eight brothers and sisters. Every Christmas my younger brother Bobby would wake up extra early and open everybody's presents - everybody's - so by the time the rest of us got up, all the gifts were shredded, ribbons off, torn open and thrown aside.

Tommy Hilfiger

"At this festive season of the year, Mr Scrooge," said the gentleman, taking up a pen, "it is more than usually desirable that we should make some slight provision for the poor and destitute, who suffer greatly at the present time. ... We choose this time, because it is a time, of all others, when Want is keenly felt, and Abundance rejoices.

Charles Dickens

I might do 'X Factor' next year. It's looking good that I won't get the sack at Christmas.

Gary Barlow

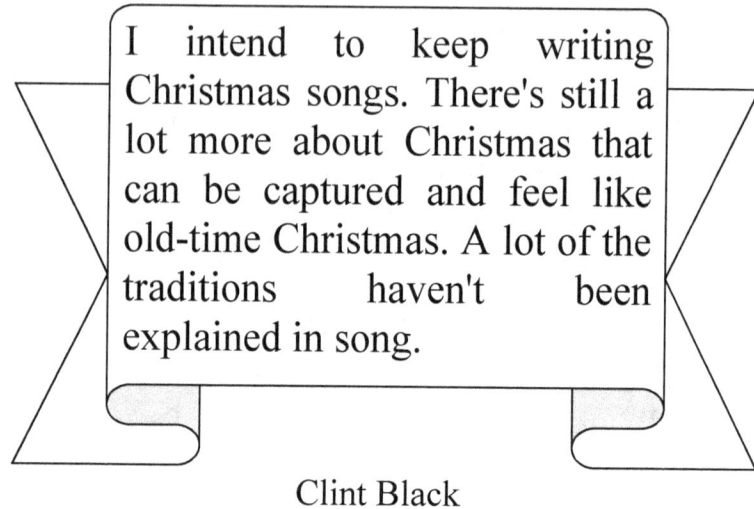

I intend to keep writing Christmas songs. There's still a lot more about Christmas that can be captured and feel like old-time Christmas. A lot of the traditions haven't been explained in song.

Clint Black

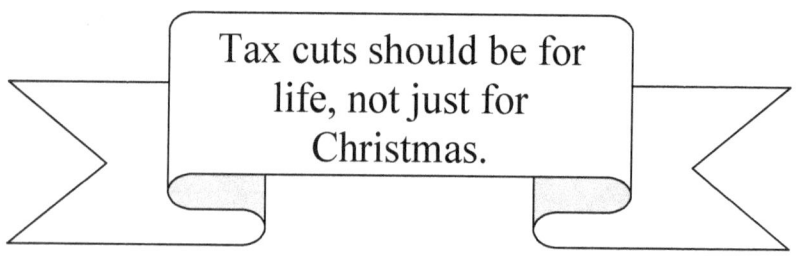

Tax cuts should be for life, not just for Christmas.

George Osborne

Godot is whatever it is in life that you are waiting for: 'I'm waiting to win the lottery. I'm waiting to fall in love'. For me, as a child, it was Christmas. At least that eventually came.

Ian Mckellen

It is Christmas in the heart that puts Christmas in the air.

W. T. Ellis

The best of all gifts around any Christmas tree: the presence of a happy family all wrapped up in each other.

Burton Hillis

I'm one of those people who had Christmas and my birthday always combined, and generally, my birthday was pretty much ignored. But my parents are always good about making some kind of special effort to make me feel like I also have a birthday that exists.

Noel Wells

I was Christmas shopping and ran into a guy on the street. I noticed his watch and said that it runs slow. He said, "So does the guy I stole it from."

David Letterman

Christmas to a child is the first terrible proof that to travel hopefully is better than to arrive.

Stephen Fry

Christmas gift suggestions:
To your enemy, forgiveness.
To an opponent, tolerance.
To a friend, your heart.
To a customer, service.
To all, charity.
To every child, a good example.
To yourself, respect.

Oren Arnold

Making a Christmas album is looked upon by some people as the thing you do when you are heading towards retirement.

Annie Lennox

Christmas makes everything twice as sad.

Douglas Coupland

My favorite traditional Christmas movie that I like to watch is All Quiet on the Western Front. It's just not December without that movie in my house.

Tom Hanks

A Christmas candle is a lovely thing;
It makes no noise at all,
But softly gives itself away;
While quite unselfish, it grows small.

Eva K. Logue

I can't tell you how scary it can be walking onto a movie and suddenly joining this family, it's like going to somebody else's Christmas dinner, everyone knows everyone, and you're there and you're not quite sure what you're supposed to be doing.

John Cleese

Blessed is the season which engages the whole world in a conspiracy of love!

Hamilton Wright Mabie

In the old days, it was not called the Holiday Season; the Christians called it 'Christmas' and went to church; the Jews called it 'Hanukkah' and went to synagogue; the atheists went to parties and drank. People passing each other on the street would say 'Merry Christmas!' or 'Happy Hanukkah!' or (to the atheists) 'Look out for the wall!'

Dave Barry

The only real
blind person at
Christmas-time
is he who has
not Christmas in
his heart.

Helen Keller

I was a postman
one   Christmas
and I developed
a morbid fear of
dogs.

Diane Abbott

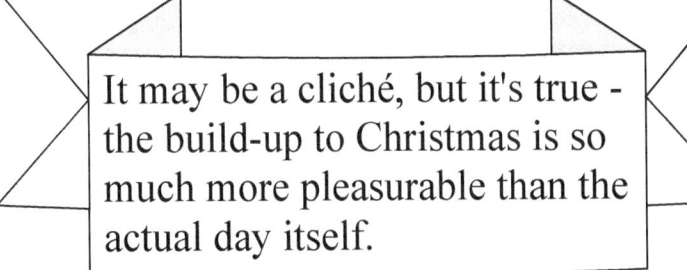

It may be a cliché, but it's true - the build-up to Christmas is so much more pleasurable than the actual day itself.

Julie Burchill

Christmas begins about the first of December with an office party and ends when you finally realize what you spent, around April fifteenth of the next year.

P. J. O'Rourke

Once again we find ourselves enmeshed in the Holiday Season, that very special time of year when we join with our loved ones in sharing centuries-old traditions such as trying to find a parking space at the mall. We traditionally do this in my family by driving around the parking lot until we see a shopper emerge from the mall, then we follow her, in very much the same spirit as the Three Wise Men, who 2,000 years ago followed a star, week after week, until it led them to a parking space.

Dave Barry

For a Jewish guy, I've recorded a lot of Christmas albums.

Barry Manilow

Yet as I read the birth stories about Jesus I cannot help but conclude that though the world may be tilted toward the rich and powerful, God is tilted toward the underdog.

Philip Yancey

May I share with you my earliest memory of a political row? It was with my mother, about the Queen - classic Freudian stuff, shrinks would say. I was eight, and refusing to watch the Queen's Christmas Day broadcast.

Alastair Campbell

At Christmas
A man is at his finest towards the finish
of the year;
He is almost what he should be when
the Christmas season's here;
Then he's thinking more of others than
he's thought the months before,
And the laughter of his children is a joy
worth toiling for.
He is less a selfish creature than at any
other time;
When the Christmas spirit rules him he
comes close to the sublime.

Edgar Guest

You know you're getting old, when
Santa starts looking younger.

Robert Paul

The whole point of me doing a Christmas record and what I centered it around was the song 'Christmas with You' from the point-of-view of the soldiers in Iraq.

Rick Springfield

I like, 'I Believe In Father Christmas' - that is one of my favorites it is a lovely composition; 'Colder Than Winter' as well. There are so many beautiful songs.

Sarah Brightman

In 1934, the American Jewish charities offered to find homes for 300 German refugee children. We were on the SS Washington, bound for New York, Christmas 1934.

Jack Steinberger

Christmas is most truly Christmas when we celebrate it by giving the light of love to those who need it most.

Ruth Carter Stapleton

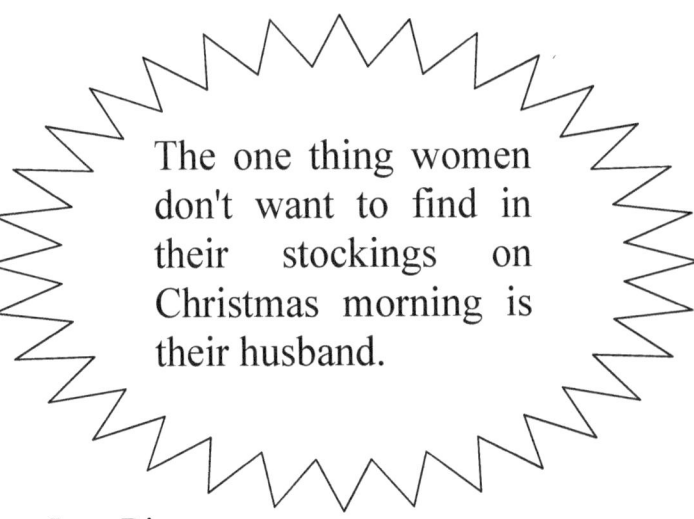

The one thing women don't want to find in their stockings on Christmas morning is their husband.

Joan Rivers

No matter where I am in the world, I will always be back home for Christmas.

Malaika Arora Khan

One of the most glorious messes in the world is the mess created in the living room on Christmas day. Don't clean it up too quickly.

Andy Rooney

I simply believe food is too good to throw away - and Christmas leftovers can be a gastronomic opportunity for the well-skilled kitchen forager. With a little imagination, there are a million ways to use up leftovers rather than bin them.

Tristram Stuart

Christmas is the season when people run out of money before they run out of friends.

Larry Wilde

I started when I was 6 years old. My brother and sister would get all of these presents at Christmas time from the cast and crew of their show and I was jealous. So I decided that I had to become an actor.

Sara Gilbert

Christmas Eve was a night of song that wrapped itself about you like a shawl. But it warmed more than your body. It warmed your heart...filled it, too, with melody that would last forever.

Bess Streeter Aldrich

Christmas is a time when everybody wants his past forgotten and his present remembered. What I don't like about office Christmas parties is looking for a job the next day.

Phyllis Diller

My father died when I was young and I was raised by my grandmother, Emma Klonjlaleh Brown. We could afford to eat chicken just once a year, on Christmas.

George Weah

Christmas! The very word brings joy to our hearts. No matter how we may dread the rush, the long Christmas lists for gifts and cards to be bought and given-when Christmas Day comes there is still the same warm feeling we had as children, the same warmth that enfolds our hearts and our homes.

Joan Winmill Brown

There are some people who want to throw their arms round you simply because it is Christmas; there are other people who want to strangle you simply because it is Christmas.

Robert Lynd

With a track like 'White Christmas,' everybody has done that song in every format you can imagine, so I just looked at the chords at that particular song and what chords would make it work. That's kind of quite a sad song, and I had this idea of someone singing it in the subway, someone who is homeless, old and sad.

Vince Clarke

I once bought my kids a set of batteries for Christmas with a note on it saying, toys not included.

Bernard Manning

I wish we could put up some of the Christmas spirit in jars and open a jar of it every month.

Harlan Miller

Christmas is doing a little something extra for someone.

Charles Schulz

The cheese board is my big treat at Christmas that I have to deny myself during the rest of year.

Johnny Vegas

The Supreme Court has ruled that they cannot have a nativity scene in Washington, D.C. This wasn't for any religious reasons. They couldn't find three wise men and a virgin.

Jay Leno

Snowflakes swirl down gently in the deep blue haze beyond the window.
The outside world is a dream
Inside, the fireplace is brightly lit, and the Yule log crackles with orange and crimson sparks.
There's a steaming mug in your hands, warming your fingers.
There's a friend seated across from you in the cozy chair, warming your heart.
There is mystery unfolding.

Vera Nazarian

Christmas is the keeping-place for memories of our innocence.

Joan Mills

I became hugely overweight and then hated myself because it was a form of self-abuse, something over which I had no control. I think the thing compulsive over-eaters want to achieve is that stuffed-full Christmas afternoon feeling.

Marcus Brigstocke

As long as we know in our hearts what Christmas *ought* to be, Christmas *is*.

Eric Severeid

From a commercial point of view, if Christmas did not exist it would be necessary to invent it.

Katharine Whitehorn

Every Christmas should begin with the sound of bells, and when I was a child mine always did. But they were sleigh bells, not church bells, for we lived in a part of Cedar Rapids, Iowa, where there were no churches.

Paul Engle

As a very young man growing up in Texas, usually I got a shotgun or cowboy boots for Christmas.

Robert Wilson

We no longer sing and dance. We don't know how to. Instead, we watch other people sing and dance on the television screen. Christmas, which was once a festival of active enjoyment, has turned into a binge of purely passive pleasures.

Tom Hodgkinson

Most of the soap operas always use the Christmas special to kill huge quantities of their characters. So they have trams coming off their rails, or cars slamming into each other or burning buildings. It's a general clean-out.

Julian Fellowes

It snowed last year too: I made a snowman and my brother knocked it down and I knocked my brother down and then we had tea.

Dylan Thomas

I stood for almost an hour in a line of shuffling, bitter-eyed late mailers (Christmas is such a carefree, low - pressure time - that's one of the things I love about it).

Stephen King

The rooms were very still while the pages were softly turned and the winter sunshine crept in to touch the bright heads and serious faces with a Christmas greeting.

Louisa May Alcott

The real reason Jews don't have more Hanukkah music is that, historically, American Jewish singer-songwriters were too busy making Christmas music. 'White Christmas,' 'Rudolph the Red-Nosed Reindeer,' 'Silver Bells' and 'The Christmas Song (Chestnuts Roasting)' were all written by Jews.

Matisyahu

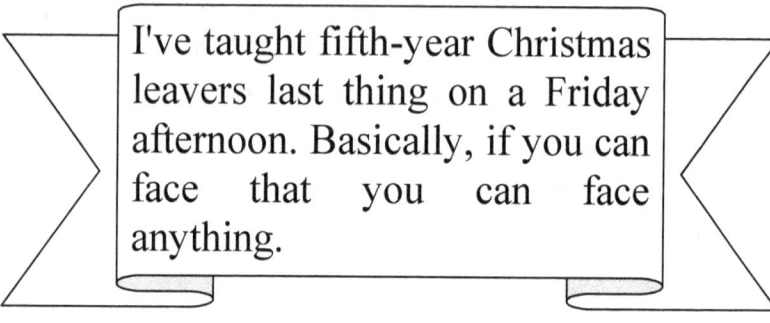

I've taught fifth-year Christmas leavers last thing on a Friday afternoon. Basically, if you can face that you can face anything.

Johann Lamont

The unfortunate thing about working for yourself is that you have the worst boss in the world. I work every day of the year except at Christmas, when I work a half day.

David Eddings

From a very young age, I liked to take apart things. All of my Christmas gifts would wind up in a million pieces. I actually recall taking apart my dad's lawnmower three times to understand how combustible engines work.

Homaro Cantu

I started my career in politics in 1967. I'm not new to this. I did not just fall off the Christmas tree. I understand the world is complex. I know that there are people out there who want to hurt other people.

Dennis Kucinich

South Park started as a little video Christmas card.

Joel Hodgson

It's fun when you start a movie, because it's kind of like you get to go Christmas shopping... you get to make your wish list and you start thinking about what each character needs.

Spike Jonze

What do you call people who are afraid of Santa Claus? Claustrophobic."

Unknown

I played guitar from the age of four or five. Every year there would be a slightly larger triangular box under the Christmas tree, until finally I got one that was big enough to make a proper sound.

Johnny Marr

So many people release albums before Christmas and they get lost in the Christmas rush.

Bonnie Tyler

One of my favorite movies of all time is 'It's A Wonderful Life,' which is a pretty interesting choice for a seasonal Christmas favorite, because it's about a guy who wants to commit suicide and is presented with reasons not to.

Frank Darabont

Our last jam session was this past Christmas. Dad played his harmonica, Mom sang in English and Italian, and I played guitar. I'm so happy that we could share that musical experience for one last time.

Tony Visconti

Christmas is for children. But it is for grownups too. Even if it is a headache, a chore, and nightmare, it is a period of necessary defrosting of chill and hide-bound hearts.

Lenora Mattingly Weber

Did you know that Christmas Day is absolutely the best day to fly? It is. No crowded airports and crowded planes. I always flew to Australia. That's what Christmas was for me - a plane journey to the next tournament.

Monica Seles

'Twas Christmas broach'd the mightiest ale;
'Twas Christmas told the merriest tale;
A Christmas gambol oft could cheer
The poor man's heart through half the year.

Sir Walter Scott

A typical Christmas is me shucking oysters. I love them and I always get them in at Christmas.

Hugh Bonneville

Christmas is the gentlest, loveliest festival of the revolving year - and yet, for all that, when it speaks, its voice has strong authority.

W.J. Cameron

In our racist, sexist society, Christmas is the eight hours when we stop killing each other and gratuitous overeating is encouraged so that the starving and other people in the world can die!

Lloyd Kaufman

Christmas was always a big holiday in our family. Every Christmas Eve before we'd go to bed, my mom and dad would read to us two or three stories and they would always be 'The Happy Prince,' 'The Gift of the Magi' and 'Twas the Night Before Christmas,' and I would like to keep that alive.

Cameron Mathison

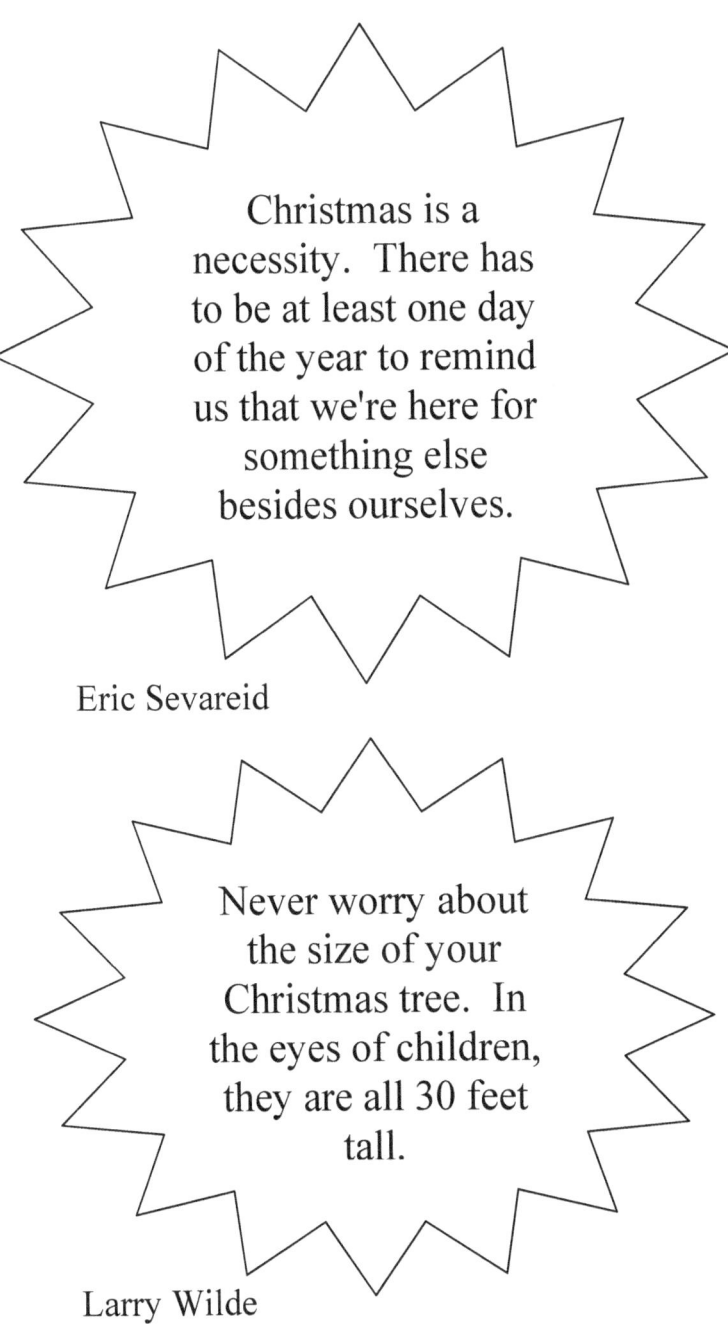

Christmas is a
necessity. There has
to be at least one day
of the year to remind
us that we're here for
something else
besides ourselves.

Eric Sevareid

Never worry about
the size of your
Christmas tree. In
the eyes of children,
they are all 30 feet
tall.

Larry Wilde

Christmas was always a big holiday in our family. Every Christmas Eve before we'd go to bed, my mom and dad would read to us two or three stories and they would always be 'The Happy Prince,' 'The Gift of the Magi' and 'Twas the Night Before Christmas,' and I would like to keep that alive.

Cameron Mathison

In the spring of 1994 I decided not to seek re-election to the Senate. I had made the decision 12 years earlier, Christmas Day of 1982, just after I had been first elected to a full term,that I would do the best I could for a limited time.

George J. Mitchell

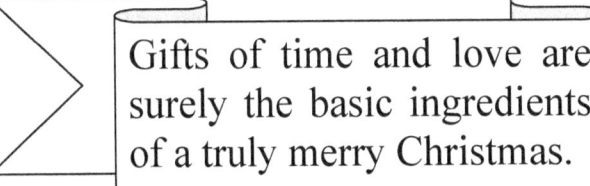

Gifts of time and love are surely the basic ingredients of a truly merry Christmas.

Peg Bracken

Christmas is forever, not for
just one day,
For loving, sharing, giving, are
not to put away
Like bells and lights and tinsel,
in some box upon a shelf.
The good you do for others is
good you do yourself...

Norman Wesley Brooks

I'd just got back from filming my role as Flo in 'Kidnap & Ransom' when I got the news that Channel 4 had re-commissioned 'Fresh Meat,' so I think it was the first Christmas I could actually relax knowing that I had three months' work sorted. As an actor, that's always a good feeling.

Kimberley Nixon

At Christmas, it's my siblings running around the house, we're cooking, talking, laughing, loud and just crazy. It's beautiful chaos.

Tika Sumpter

Christmas is a time when kids tell Santa what they want and adults pay for it. Deficits are when adults tell the government what they want and their kids pay for it.

Richard Lamm

A lot of sequins for New Year's! Red, green, white - I fail at all of that because I'm always in black. But for Christmas, I do love wearing cute dresses with tights and a pair of boots.

Ashley Benson

I do like Christmas on the whole...In its clumsy way, it does approach Peace and Goodwill. But it is clumsier every year.

E.M. Forster

Christmas is a spirit that flows from one heart to another. It is more precious than rubies and better than gold.

Agnes M. Pharo

Why not collect and clean chicken wishbones in the run-up to Christmas, spray them silver and use each to pinch together a white hem-stitch napkin?

Pippa Middleton

Christmas is the season when you buy this year's gifts with next year's money.

Unknown

Christmas movies, it's a hard thing to do. The danger is you just end up with a Hollywood star with a Santa beard. You risk it being fake and cheesy and not real.

Peter Baynham

There is a remarkable breakdown of taste and intelligence at Christmastime. Mature, responsible grown men wear neckties made of holly leaves and drink alcoholic beverages with raw egg yolks and cottage cheese in them.

P.J. O'Rourke

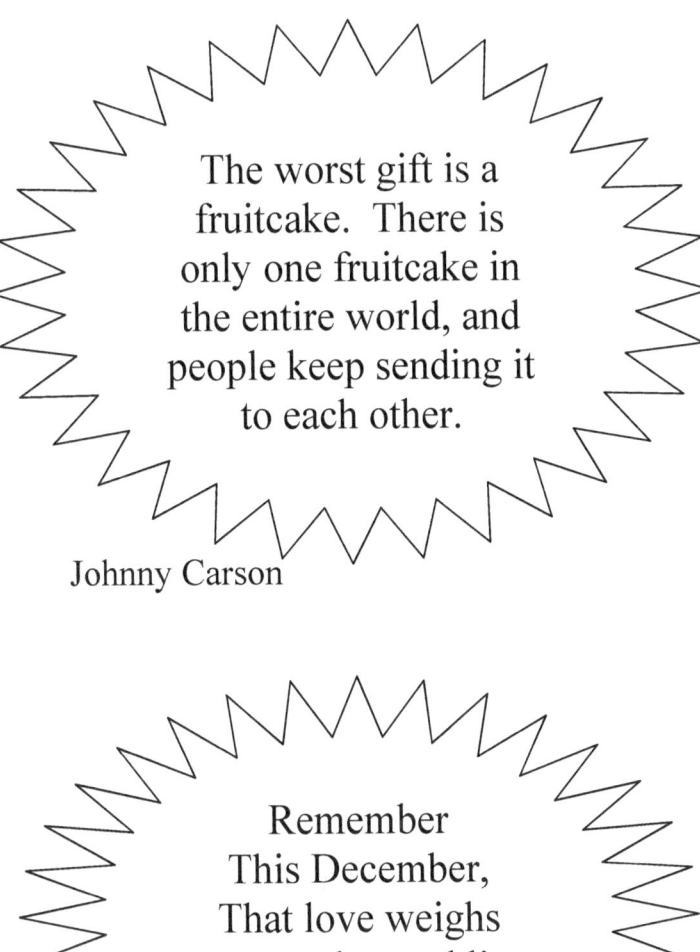

The worst gift is a fruitcake. There is only one fruitcake in the entire world, and people keep sending it to each other.

Johnny Carson

Remember
This December,
That love weighs
more than gold!

Josephine Dodge Daskam Bacon

For the spirit of Christmas fulfils the greatest hunger of mankind.

Loring A. Schuler

When I was eight, my mum found me humming to myself and scribbling on a scrap of paper. When she asked me what I was doing, I got shy. I was writing a Christmas song, and I had never shared my music with anyone before. Reluctantly, I sang it for her... and she loved it. Of course she did - she's my mum.

Neil Jackson

I can understand people simply fleeing the mountainous effort Christmas has become... but there are always a few saving graces and finally they make up for all the bother and distress.

May Sarton

Next to a circus there ain't nothing that packs up and tears out faster than the Christmas spirit.

Kin Hubbard

I never believed in Santa Claus because I knew no white dude would come into my neighborhood after dark.

Dick Gregory

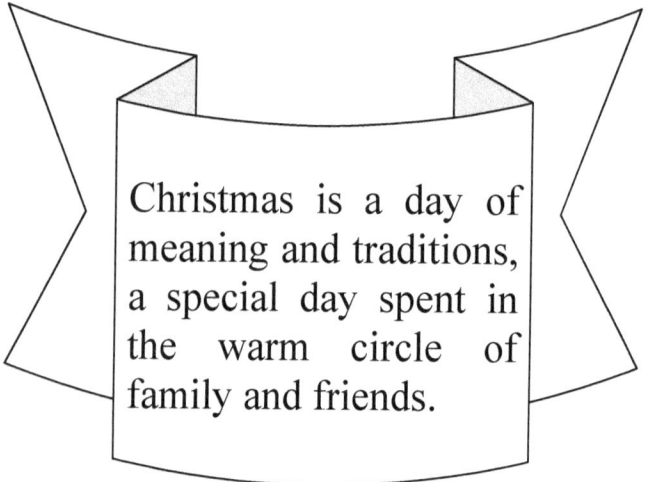

Christmas is a day of meaning and traditions, a special day spent in the warm circle of family and friends.

Margaret Thatcher

Which Christmas is the most vivid to me? It's always the next Christmas.

Joanne Woodward

Although it is pleasant to think about poison at any season, there is something special about Christmas, and I found myself grinning.

Alan Bradley, *I Am Half-Sick of Shadows*

The Christmas spirit - love -
changes hearts and lives.

Pat Boone

Not believe in Santa Claus!
You might as well not believe
in fairies!

Francis Pharcellus Church

Easter in snow,
Christmas in mud;
Christmas in snow,
Easter in mud.

Old English saying

White Easter
brings green
Christmas.

Old English saying

Christmas is a time when people of all religions come together to worship Jesus Christ.

Bart Simpson

Something about an old-fashioned Christmas is hard to forget.

Hugh Downs

There are some wonderful aspects to Christmas. It's magical. And each year, from at least November, well, September, well, if I'm honest, May, I look forward to it hugely.

Miranda Hart

At Christmas, all roads lead home.

Marjorie Holmes

It was the beginning of the greatest Christmas ever. Little food. No presents. But there was a snowman in their basement.

Markus Zusak, *The Book Thief*

Ever since the Christmas of '53, I have felt that the yuletide is a special hell for those families who have suffered any loss or who must admit to any imperfection; the so-called spirit of giving can be as greedy as receiving - Christmas is our time to be aware of what we lack, of who's not home.

John Irving

What kind of Christmas present would Jesus ask Santa for?

Salman Rushdie

I know what I really want for Christmas. I want my childhood back. Nobody is going to give me that. I might give at least the memory of it to myself if I try. I know it doesn't make sense, but since when is Christmas about sense, anyway? It is about a child, of long ago and far away, and it is about the child of now. In you and me. Waiting behind the door of or hearts for something wonderful to happen. A child who is impractical, unrealistic, simpleminded and terribly vulnerable to joy.

Robert Fulghum

Were I a philosopher, I should write a philosophy of toys, showing that nothing else in life need to be taken seriously, and that Christmas Day in the company of children is one of the few occasions on which men become entirely alive.

Robert Lynd

If ice will bear a man before Christmas, it will not bear a mouse afterward.

Old English saying

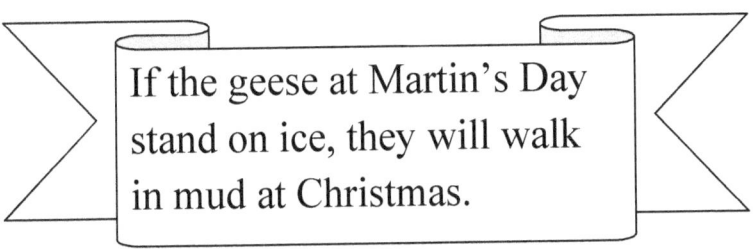

If the geese at Martin's Day stand on ice, they will walk in mud at Christmas.

Old English saying

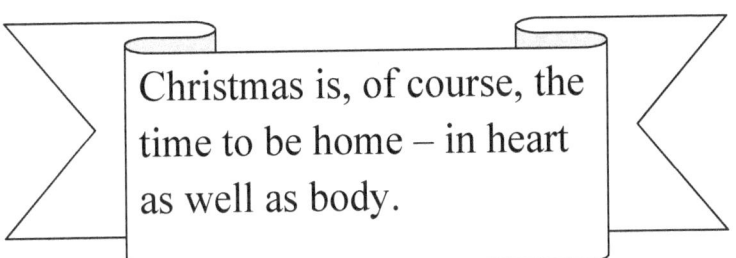

Christmas is, of course, the time to be home – in heart as well as body.

Garry Moore

What is Christmas? It is tenderness for the past, courage for the present, hope for the future. It is a fervent wish that every cup may overflow with blessings rich and eternal, and that every path may lead to peace.

Agnes M. Pahro

At its best, Christmas is a mirror in which we see reflected the very best life can be. Where we see ourselves moved by generosity, inspired by hope, and uplifted by love, not only for ourselves but for the whole evolving universe.

Bruce Sanguin

Blend equal parts of Faith and Hope
mixed well with Charity;
Stir in Good Will and Sweet Content
and Precious Memory.
Add Kindness, Helpfulness and Joy;
of Gratitude don't spare;
Then drop by drop Love's Essence
sweet, and Praises freely share.
And don't forget such spices rare as
Laughter, Smiles and Fun,
Taste often for the best results, ('Tis
sweet to mince upon).
Now add a
Thankful Heart and then, the recipe's
complete,
Your "Merry Christmas" all will like
… so try the season's treat.

Esther Lloyd Dauber

Are you willing to stoop down and consider the needs and desires of little children; to remember the weaknesses and loneliness of people who are growing old; to stop asking how much your friends love you, and to ask yourself if you love them enough; to bear in mind the things that other people have to bear on their hearts; to trim your lamp so that it will give more light and less smoke, and to carry it in front so that your shadow will fall behind you; to make a grave for your ugly thoughts and a garden for your kindly feelings, with the gate open? Are you willing to do these things for a day? Then you are ready to keep Christmas!

Henry van Dyke

Children sleeping, snow is softly falling
Dreams are calling like bells in the distance
We were dreamers not so long ago
But one by one we all had to grow up
When it seems the magic's slipped away
We find it all again on Christmas day.

Josh Groban

Christmas has lost its meaning for us because we have lost the spirit of expectancy. We cannot prepare for an observance. We must prepare for an experience.

Handel H. Brow

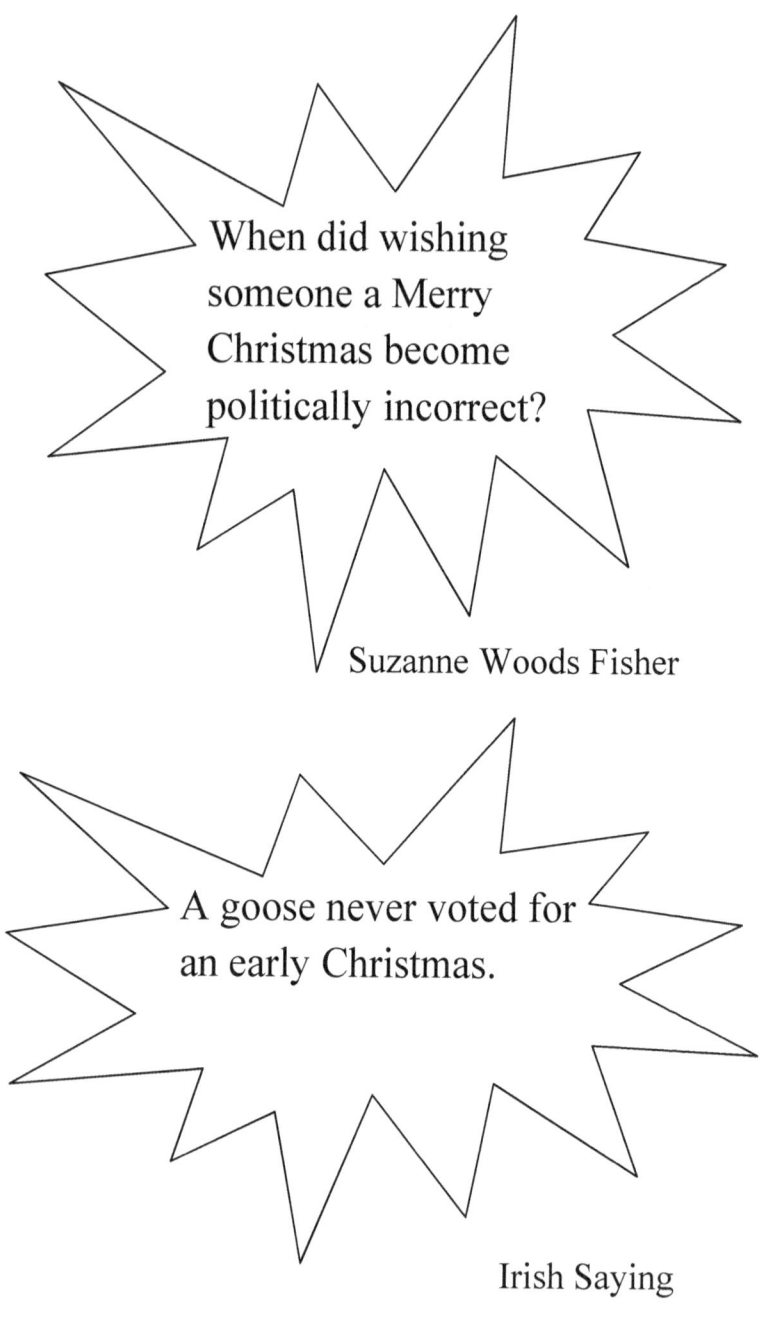

When did wishing someone a Merry Christmas become politically incorrect?

Suzanne Woods Fisher

A goose never voted for an early Christmas.

Irish Saying

Christmas is built upon a beautiful and intentional paradox; that the birth of the homeless should be celebrated in every home.

G.K. Chesterton

Do give books - religious or otherwise - for Christmas. They're never fattening, seldom sinful, and permanently personal.

Lenore Hershey

The day I saw my mom eating the Santa cookies on the plate was one of the most horrific days of my life.

Halle Berry

Even before Christmas has said Hello, it's saying 'Buy Buy',

Robert Paul

If Ifs and Buts were candies and nuts, we'd all have a merry Christmas.

Unknown

It struck him that how you spent Christmas was a message to the world about where you were in life, some indication of how deep a hole you had managed to burrow for yourself.

Nick Hornby, *About a Boy*

One good thing about Christmas shopping: it toughens you for the January sales.

Grace Kriley

One of the nice things about Christmas is that you can make people forget the past with a present.

Unknown

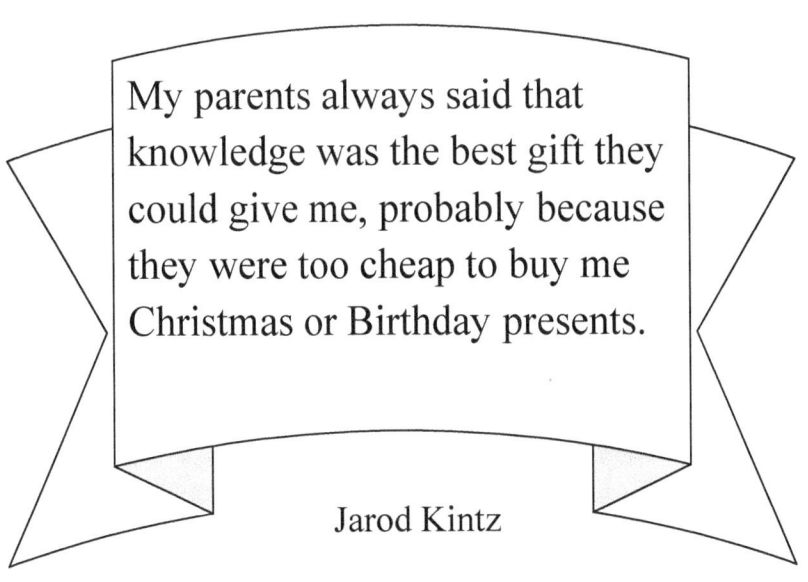

My parents always said that knowledge was the best gift they could give me, probably because they were too cheap to buy me Christmas or Birthday presents.

Jarod Kintz

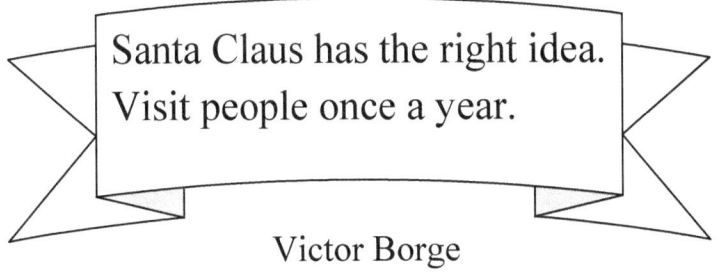

Santa Claus has the right idea. Visit people once a year.

Victor Borge

> Mankind is a great, an immense family ... This is proved by what we feel in our hearts at Christmas.

Pope John Paul XXIII

> On a busy day twenty-two thousand people come to visit Santa, and I was told that it is an elf's lot to remain merry in the face of torment and adversity. I promised to keep that in mind.

David Sedaris

Love the giver more
than the gift.

Brigham Young

Christmas is a time
when you get
homesick - even
when you're home.

Carol Nelson

My idea of Christmas, whether old-fashioned or modern, is very simple: loving others. Come to think of it, why do we have to wait for Christmas to do that?

Bob Hope

Christmas can be celebrated in the school room with pine trees, tinsel and reindeers, but there must be no mention of the man whose birthday is being celebrated. One wonders how a teacher would answer if a student asked why it was called Christmas.

Ronald Reagan

Perhaps the best Yuletide decoration is being wreathed in smiles.

Anon

From home to home, and heart to heart, from one place to another. The warmth and joy of Christmas, brings us closer to each other.

Emily Matthews

How many observe Christ's birthday! How few, His precepts!

Benjamin Franklin

Heap on the wood!-the wind is chill;
But let it whistle as it will,
We'll keep our Christmas merry still.

Sir Walter Scott

Keep your friends close, your enemies closer, and receipts for all major purchases.

Bridger Winegar

I have various snowy memories, I remember clearly getting a wonderful red bike and I remember a train set that my father set up the night before Christmas not knowing that I had secretly seen him doing it. So that was my first major acting role - having to open the box in the morning and act surprised and say, "Oh my God, a train." It was funny. He didn't catch on.

Matthew Broderick

Christmas is a state of mind and that special feeling that only comes with an empty bank account.

Melanie White

I sometimes think we expect too much of Christmas Day. We try to crowd into it the long arrears of kindliness and humanity of the whole year. As for me, I like to take my Christmas a little at a time, all through the year. And thus I drift along into the holidays - let them overtake me unexpectedly - waking up some find morning and suddenly saying to myself: 'Why, this is Christmas Day!'

Ray Stannard Baker

Are you willing to believe that love is the strongest thing in the world - stronger than hate, stronger than evil, stronger than death - and that the blessed life which began in Bethlehem nineteen hundred years ago is the image and brightness of the Eternal Love? Then you can keep Christmas.

Henry Van Dyke

Merry Christmas, nearly everybody!

Ogden Nash

A Christmas shopper's complaint is one of long-standing.

Anonymous

Our hearts grow tender with childhood memories and love of kindred, and we are better throughout the year for having, in spirit, become a child again at Christmas-time.

Laura Ingalls Wilder

Why is Christmas just like a day at the office?
You do all the work and the fat guy with the suit gets all the credit.

Anonymous

I will never forget when I was about 12, and my mother told my siblings and me that we would not be receiving Christmas gifts because there wasn't enough money. I remember at the time that I felt sad and thought: "What would I say when the other kids asked what I had gotten?" Just when I started to accept that there would not be a Christmas that year, three nuns showed up at our house with gifts for us. There was a turkey, a fruit basket, and some games, and for me, there was a doll.

Oprah Winfrey

I felt overstuffed and dull and disappointed, the way I always do the day after Christmas, as if whatever it was the pine boughs and the candles and the silver and gilt-ribboned presents and the birch-log fires and the Christmas turkey and the carols at the piano promised never came to pass.

Sylvia Plath

God is here. This truth should fill our lives, and every Christmas should be for us a new and special meeting with God, when we allow His light and grace to enter deep into our soul.

Josemaría Escrivá

Christmas works
like glue, it
keeps us all
sticking
together.

Rosie Thomas

There has been
only one
Christmas - the
rest are
anniversaries.

W. J. Cameron

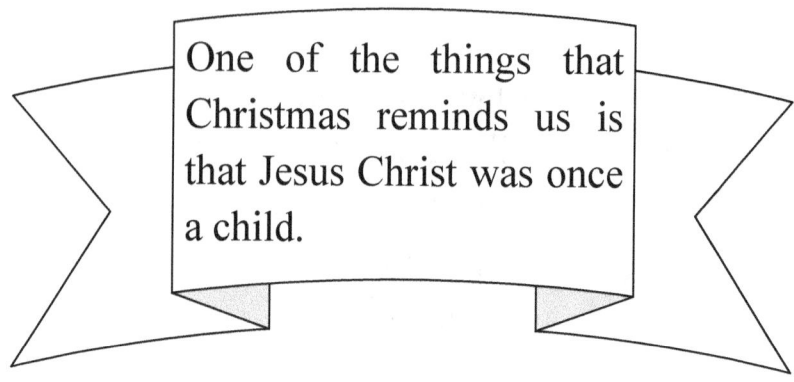

One of the things that Christmas reminds us is that Jesus Christ was once a child.

Hark Herald Sarmiento

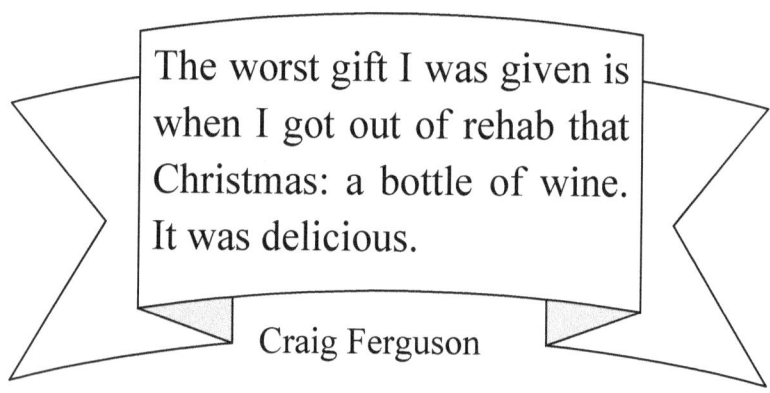

The worst gift I was given is when I got out of rehab that Christmas: a bottle of wine. It was delicious.

Craig Ferguson

Also by Alicia Brent

Resolutions & Reflections for the New Year

Sugar-Free Smoothies For The Fast Diet

Dead Interesting

Samuel Johnson Man of Words

Ellen White Speaks Out